I wish you a better life

Belangs to

_____

_____

_____

Personal Information

Full Name: ――――――――――――――――――――――――

Relevant nickname : ―――――――――――――――――――――
――――――――――――――――――――――――――――

Maiden Name (if applicable) :――――――――――――――――――

Phone Numbers:

- MOBILE : ――――――――――――――――――――――――
- HOME   : ――――――――――――――――――――――――
- OFFICE : ――――――――――――――――――――――――

Date of birth: ――――――――――――――――――――――――

Marital Status: ――――――――――――――――――――――――

Date of mariage: ―――――――――――――――――――――――

Social Security Number: ―――――――――――――――――――

Military service détails: ――――――――――――――――――――

Child 1: ―――――――――――――――――――――――――――

Child 2: ―――――――――――――――――――――――――――

Child 3: ―――――――――――――――――――――――――――

Child 4: ―――――――――――――――――――――――――――

Other information: ―――――――――――――――――――――――
――――――――――――――――――――――――――――

EXTENDED FAMILY INFORMATION

MOTHER'S NAME: --

MOTHER'S MAIDEN NAME: ---

FATHER'S NAME: --

SIBLING 1: --

SIBLING 2: --

SIBLING 3: --

SIBLING 4: --

SIBLING 5: --

GRANDCHILDREN: ---

Personal Information

Full Name: --

Relevant nickname : ---

Maiden Name (if applicable) :--

Phone Numbers:

- MOBILE : ---
- HOME   : ---
- OFFICE : ---

Date of birth: ---

Marital Status: ---

Date of mariage: ---

Social security Number: --

Military service détails: --

Child 1: ---

Child 2: ---

Child 3: ---

Child 4: ---

Other information: --

EXTENDED FAMILY INFORMATION

MOTHER'S NAME: ---

MOTHER'S MAIDEN NAME: --

FATHER'S NAME: --

SIBLING 1: ---

SIBLING 2: ---

SIBLING 3: ---

SIBLING 4: ---

SIBLING 5: ---

GRANDCHILDREN: ---

DATE :

DATE :

DATE: -------------------------------

DATE : --

DATE :

DATE :

DATE :

DATE :

DATE:

DATE : --

DATE :

DATE :

DATE :

DATE :

DATE :

DATE :

DATE :

DATE :

DATE :

DATE: --

DATE :

DATE : --------------------- ---------------

DATE :

DATE : -------------------

DATE :

DATE : --

DATE :

DATE : ---------------------------------

DATE:

DATE:

DATE :

DATE :

DATE :

DATE : ----------

DATE :

DATE :

DATE :

DATE :

DATE :

DATE:

DATE : --

DATE :

DATE :

DATE: --

DATE : --

DATE : ------------------------------------

DATE :

DATE:

DATE : --

DATE :

DATE : ----

DATE : ----------------------------------

DATE : --

DATE :

DATE : -----------------------------------

DATE :

DATE : --

DATE :

DATE :

DATE :

DATE :

DATE:

DATE :

DATE: --

DATE :

DATE :

DATE : --

DATE :

DATE : --

DATE :

DATE :

DATE :

DATE :

DATE :

DATE :

DATE:

DATE :

DATE :

DATE :

DATE :

DATE:

DATE:

DATE:

DATE : --

DATE :

DATE :

DATE :

DATE :

DATE:

DATE :

DATE: --

DATE :

DATE :

DATE :

DATE : ----------

DATE:

DATE :

DATE:

DATE :

DATE:

DATE : --

 DATE :

DATE : --------------------------------------

DATE :

DATE :

DATE :

DATE :

DATE :

DATE :

DATE :

DATE : -------------------------------------

DATE :

DATE :

DATE: --

CPSIA information can be obtained
at www.ICGtesting.com
Printed in the USA
LVHW022334161121
703493LV00005B/1019